Extreme
HISTORY

First published in 2012 by Miles Kelly
Publishing Ltd, Harding's Barn, Bardfield End
Green, Thaxted, Essex, CM6 3PX, UK

Copyright © Miles Kelly Publishing Ltd 2011

© 2014 Discovery Communications, LLC.
Discovery Explore Your World™ and the
Discovery Explore Your World™ logo are
trademarks of Discovery Communications, LLC,
used under license. All rights reserved.
discoveryuk.com

This edition published in 2014

10 9 8 7 6 5 4 3 2 1

Publishing Director Belinda Gallagher
Creative Director Jo Cowan
Managing Editors Amanda Askew,
Rosie Neave
Managing Designer Simon Lee
Proofreaders Carly Blake, Claire Philip
Production Manager Elizabeth Collins
Image Manager Liberty Newton
Reprographics Stephan Davis, Thom Allaway

ISBN 978-1-78209-529-3

Printed in China

British Library Cataloguing-in-Publication Data
A catalogue record for this book is available
from the British Library

Made with paper from a sustainable forest

www.mileskelly.net
info@mileskelly.net

ACKNOWLEDGMENTS

The publishers would like to thank the following sources for the use
of their photographs:

KEY Fotolia=F, Getty Images=GI, istockphoto.com=iS, The Moviestore Collection
Ltd=MSC, Rex Features=RF, Shutterstock=S
t=top, a=above, b=bottom/below, c=center, l=left, r=right, f=far, m=main,
bg=background

COVER James Bruntz/GI **BACK COVER** Scott Rothstein/S 1 Dan Breckwoldt/S
2 Pedro Nogueira/S 3(bg) L.Watcharapol/S (strip, left to right) Elnur/F, Dmitrijs
Mihejevs/S 4–5 Warner Bros. Pictures/Helena Productions/Latina Pictures/
Radiant Productions/Plan B Entertainment/MSC 6–7(bg)Jenny Solomon/F,
(bg, bl) Binkski/S 6(bl) 2003 Charles Walker/TopFoto, (br) Sandro Vannini/Corbis
7(bl) The Granger Collection/TopFoto, (bc) The Granger Collection/TopFoto,
(br) Studio 37/S 8–9(frame) Ladyann/S 8(m) Time & Life Pictures/GI,
(tl) grivet/S, (tr) kanate/S 9(c) 2001 Topham/PA/TopFoto, (cl) Roger-
Viollet/TopFoto, (bl) GI 12–13(bg) Hywit Dimyadi/S, (game board) Katherine
Welles/S, (map) ilolab/S, (counters) Lars Kastilan/S, (dice) Bombaert Patrick/S,
(panels) Stephen Aaron Rees/S 12(heading paper) Jakub Krechowicz/S,
(tr) Charles Walker/TopFoto, (cl) Bettmann/Corbis, (bl) National Geographic/GI
13(tl) Bettmann/Corbis, (tr) GI, (bl) GI, (br) Popperfoto/GI
14–5(bg) pashabo/S, (postcard) ronstik/S, (stamps) vesves/S, (colored pins)
oriori/S 14(tr) Patryk Kosmider/S, (bl) 2005 TopFoto, (br) Historical Picture
Archive/Corbis 15(tl) Michael Nicholson/Corbis, (tr) Print Collector/HIP/TopFoto,
(bl) The Granger Collection/TopFoto, (br) De Agostini/GI
16–7(t,l–r) ClassicStock/TopFoto, Luisa Ricciarini/TopFoto, Corbis,
ullsteinbild/TopFoto, 2002 Topham/UPP/TopFoto, (b, l–r) GI, Bettmann/Corbis,
Stapleton/HIP/TopFoto, RIA Novosti/TopFoto, Topham Picturepoint/TopFoto
18–9(bg) Cindi L/S 18(t) O.V.D./S 19(tr) National Geographic/GI 20–1(bg) Eky
Studio/S, (book) charles taylor/S, (blood) robybret/S, (panels) Christopher
Hudson/iS 20(l) Bettmann/Corbis, (tr) The Granger Collection/TopFoto,
(br) Print Collector/HIP/TopFoto 21(tl) The Granger Collection/TopFoto,
(tr) Ullstein Bild/TopFoto, (bl) TopFoto, (br) AFP/GI 22(cl) Maslov Dmitry/S,
(cr) Bettmann/Corbis, (bl) Bettmann/Corbis, (br) Anna Hoychuk/S
23(tl) KUCO/S, (tr) Charles Walker/TopFoto, (bl) World History Archive/TopFoto,
(br) Topham/AP/TopFoto 24–5(blood) Steve Collender/S, (fire) Sergey
Mironov/S 24(tr) SuperStock/GI, (b) GI 25(t, bg) JeremyRichards/S,
(t) Historical Picture Archive/Corbis, (bl) TopFoto 26–7(bg) zhanna ocheret/S,
(book) Evgenia Sh./S 26(tl) optimarc/S, (cl) GI, (cr) Mary Evans Picture
Library/Alamy, (bl) Studio DMM Photography, Designs & Art/S,
(br) ullsteinbild/TopFoto 27(tl) The Granger Collection/ TopFoto, (tr) GI,
(tr, fan) Margo Harrison/S, (bl) PoodlesRock/Corbis, (br) GI 28–9(bg) val
lawless/S, (bg, stains) Picsfive/S, (c) Bochkarev Photography/S
28(header panel) Sibear/S, (tr, sock) Antonov Roman/S, (tr, bowl) Ron Zmiri/S,
(blue napkins) Arogant/S, (white napkins) Lim Yong Hian/S, (folded napkins)
Tobik/S, (knife and spoon) Natalia Klenova/S, (wooden spoon) Nekrasov
Andrey/S 29(tl, plate) Kulish Viktoriia/S, (tl, mouse) marina ljubanovic/S,
(tl, sugar mouse) Lucie Lang/S, (tr, ostrich) Timo Jaakonaho/RF, (tr, camel)
mmattner/S, (tr, kebab) S, (c) Martina I. Meyer/S, (cr, glass) jesterlsv/S,
(cr, tankard) Peter Lorimer/S, (cr, mug) Lipowski Milan/S, (bl) Sergey
Shcherbakoff/S, (bc) Lagui/S, (br) discpicture/S 30–1(bg) L.Watcharapol/S
30(tl) Vitaly Korovin/S, (tl, chain text) Steve Collender/S, (tr) Chyrko Olena/S,
(l) Picsfive/S, (cr) Gianni Dagli Orti/Corbis, (bl) The Gallery Collection/Corbis,
(br) pandapaw/S, (br, panel) Vitaly Korovin/S 31(tl) David Burrows/S,
(tl, window) Lusoimages/S, (tc) GI, (tc, panel) Matthias Pahl/S, (tr) noose)
Iwona Grodzka/S, (tr, ear) Washington Post/GI, (cl) M.E. Mulder/S, (cr) Charles
Walker/TopFoto, (bl) William Attard McCarthy/S, (br) ID1974/S 32–3(bg) charles
taylor/S, (nails) dusan964/S, (tags) val lawless/S 32(tr, candle) Litvinenko
Anastasia/S, (tr, teeth) Le Do/S, (cr, hot cups) Mary Evans Picture Library/Alamy,
(cr, books) Brocreative/S, (bl) Roger-Viollet/RF, (bc) SPbPhoto/S, (br, bottle)
Lakhesis/S, (br, cups) Coprid/S 33(tl) The Granger Collection/TopFoto,
(tl, leeches) Mircea Bezergheanu/S, (tc) Steve Lovegrove/S, (tr) Classic
Image/Alamy, (r) terekhov igor/S, (cl, bottles) Milos Luzanin/S, (cl, mortar and
pestle) Pshenichka/S, (cl, spices) Noraluca013/S, (cr) eduard ionescu/S,
(bl) Noam Armonn/S, (br) Mary Evans Picture Library/Alamy, (br, bg) F
34–5(t, bg) Rêmi Cauzid/S, (b, bg) zhu difeng/S, (mud) Ultrashock/S,
(tl, panel) photocell/S, (cl, panel) Excellent backgrounds Here/S, (t, l–r) GI,
Fotomas/TopFoto, Museum of London/HIP/TopFoto, (b, l–r) Hank Frentz/S,
Popperfoto/GI, Corbis 34(br, frame) kak2s/S 35(b, frame) SuriyaPhoto/S
36–7(bg) jayfish/S, (panels) Hintau Aliaksei/S 36(header panel) Raia/S,
(t) irin-k/S, (c) Ewa Walicka/S, (bl, sacks) Dee Golden, (bl, glasses) Saveliev
Alexey Alexsandrovich/S, (bc) Dreamworks/Everett/RF 37(tl) The Gallery
Collection/Corbis, (tr, mud) Ultrashock/S, (tr, helmet) bocky/S, (cl) Mettus/S,
(cr) TopFoto, (bc) Leigh Prather/S, (br) AP/Topham, (br, bg) Ana de Sousa/S
38–9(panels) Dim Dimich/S, (scrolls) koya979/S 38(header panel) inxti/S,
(bg) Kompaniets Taras/S, (tr) The Granger Collection/TopFoto (bl) Andrey
Burmakin/S 39(tl) Sophy R./S, (tr) papa1266/S, (tc, silkworms) holbox/S,
(tc, scroll) Roman Sigaev/S, (tc, gun) Kellis/S, (c) PaulPaladin/S,
(cr) Bettmann/Corbis, (bl) composite image: StudioSmart/S, PhotoHouse/S,
(br) Molodec/S

All other photographs are from: Corel, digitalSTOCK, digitalvision,
Dreamstime.com, Fotolia.com, iStockphoto.com, John Foxx, PhotoAlto,
PhotoDisc, PhotoEssentials, PhotoPro, Stockbyte

Every effort has been made to acknowledge the source and copyright
holder of each picture. The publishers apologise for any unintentional
errors or omissions.

Extreme HISTORY

Stewart Ross
Consultant: Philip Steele

Miles Kelly

CONTENTS

Living Dead	6
Battle Beasts	8
Extreme Siege	10
Fame and Fortune	12
Wonders of the World	14
Heroes and Villains	16
Great Warriors	18
Lost Leaders	20
Wipe Out!	22
Supreme Sacrifice	24
Fancy Dress	26
Rat-atouille	28
Fitting the Crime	30
Cure or Kill	32
Slumdogs and Millionaires	34
War and Peace	36
Crazy Acts	38
Index	40

◀ The movie *Troy* (2004) tells the story of the Trojan War—the ancient Greeks believed a great war, lasting for ten years, was fought in the 1200s BC between the Greeks and the Trojans.

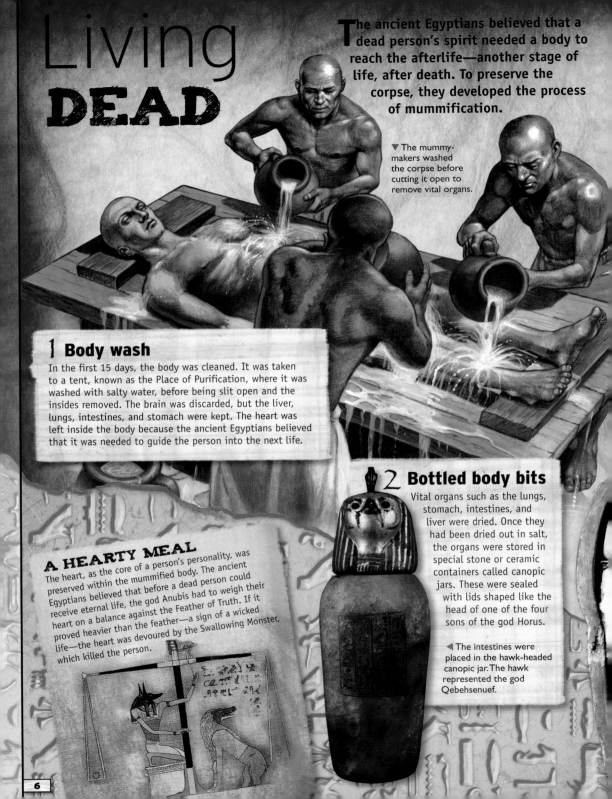

Living
DEAD

The ancient Egyptians believed that a dead person's spirit needed a body to reach the afterlife—another stage of life, after death. To preserve the corpse, they developed the process of mummification.

▼ The mummy-makers washed the corpse before cutting it open to remove vital organs.

1 Body wash

In the first 15 days, the body was cleaned. It was taken to a tent, known as the Place of Purification, where it was washed with salty water, before being slit open and the insides removed. The brain was discarded, but the liver, lungs, intestines, and stomach were kept. The heart was left inside the body because the ancient Egyptians believed that it was needed to guide the person into the next life.

A HEARTY MEAL

The heart, as the core of a person's personality, was preserved within the mummified body. The ancient Egyptians believed that before a dead person could receive eternal life, the god Anubis had to weigh their heart on a balance against the Feather of Truth. If it proved heavier than the feather—a sign of a wicked life—the heart was devoured by the Swallowing Monster, which killed the person.

2 Bottled body bits

Vital organs such as the lungs, stomach, intestines, and liver were dried. Once they had been dried out in salt, the organs were stored in special stone or ceramic containers called canopic jars. These were sealed with lids shaped like the head of one of the four sons of the god Horus.

◄ The intestines were placed in the hawk-headed canopic jar. The hawk represented the god Qebehsenuef.

3 Drying out

To prevent the flesh from rotting over time, all the moisture needed to be removed. Mummy-makers stuffed the corpse with a special salt called natron, before placing it in a natron-filled bath for 40 days. The body became shriveled, hard, and blue-black in color.

◀ The corpse is covered in natron—up to 500 lb (225 kg)—to draw out all the moisture.

1 Head wrapped and Eye of Horus placed over the slit where the organs were removed

2 Body and limbs wrapped

3 Whole body wrapped

4 Bandaging complete

5 Enclosed in canvas sheet

4 Well wrapped

After the natron was removed, the dried-out (desiccated) corpse was oiled and given false eyes and a wig to make it appear more lifelike. Then a resin was poured over the corpse to set it hard and stop mold from growing. Finally, the body was stuffed with linen and even sawdust, then wrapped in 50 ft (15 m) of linen bandages over 15 prayer-filled days.

◀ The five-stage sequence of wrapping the body always started with the head. During the wrapping, lucky amulets were placed between the bandages to protect the person from harm in the afterlife.

5 Precious possessions

Finally the preserved body was placed inside a wooden case. As death was seen as a temporary break in life, mummies were buried with everyday items such as jewelry, clothing, shoes, musical instruments, and furniture. Pet cats and dogs were also mummified to keep their owners company in the afterlife.

◀ Expensive coffins were shaped like a person and decorated with spells. Bodily features such as eyes helped the person to transfer into the afterlife.

▶ This mummy was found after 4,000 years. Its features are still recognizable because of the preservation techniques of the ancient Egyptians.

Battle BEASTS

During early warfare, commanders used a variety of animals to gain an edge over their enemy. The most common was the horse—it carried cavalry, pulled chariots, and transported heavy loads. The camel, though slower, served well in desert campaigns. By far the most spectacular warrior animal was the mighty elephant, a living tank that trampled and terrorized its foes across Asia, North Africa, and Southern Europe.

▼ In 218 BC, the Carthaginian general Hannibal launched a surprise attack on his Roman enemies by leading an army, backed by war-trained elephants, across the Alps and into Italy. Hannibal won three great victories before he was forced to retire.

Anti-elephant

Ears flapping, trunk raised, tusks lancing... the awesome sight of a war elephant on the charge was enough to turn the legs of the bravest warrior to jelly. However, tactics were devised to halt the 30-mph (50-km/h) onslaught. The Romans learned to step aside at the last minute, Alexander the Great's men slashed at the beasts' hamstrings with axes, the Mongols catapulted rocks at them, and in more modern times the beasts were brought down by cannon fire.

Charge!

While several peoples of Central Asia were renowned for being able to shoot arrows accurately while on horseback, it was only with the invention of the stirrup in the 4th century AD that cavalry came into their own. Their grandest form was the mounted medieval knight. Although no longer armored, cavalry remained a vital element of warfare well into the 20th century.

▲ About 650 British soldiers on horseback charged into enemy fire in the Battle of Balaclava, 1854. More than 240 were killed or wounded. The event was commemorated in Alfred Lord Tennyson's poem of 1854, *The Charge of the Light Brigade.*

▲ During World War I (1914–1918), dogs were not only used to deliver messages, but also to transport machine guns.

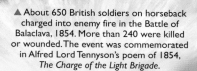

▲ G. I. Joe, part of the United States Army Pigeon Service, is decorated for valiant service in World War II (1939–1945). He delivered a message about an imminent bombing, perhaps saving more than 1,000 lives.

Woof and wing

Humans are slow and vulnerable message carriers. Before it was possible to send messages by radio, there was no better way of quickly delivering long-range information than tying it to the leg of a carrier pigeon; and no one could beat a messenger dog when it came to bounding over treacherous terrain.

THE U.S. NAVY ONCE TRAINED DOLPHINS TO SEEK OUT FROGMEN WHO WERE TRYING TO BREACH THE SECURITY AROUND SHIPS AND BASES.

Camel corps

The Imperial Camel Corps (1916–1918) was manned by British, Indian, Australian, and New Zealand riders and served with distinction in the Middle East during World War I (1914–1918). The camel's ability to go for five days without water made it ideal for desert operations.

Extreme
SIEGE

A medieval castle was an uncompromising symbol of the owner's power, might, and majesty, and if it fell, their importance and prestige tumbled with it. The masterbuilder's task, therefore, was to use every possible form of defense, from crenellations to moats, to make it as impregnable as possible. Outside, attackers devised whatever means they could to break through the stronghold.

Trebuchet The gravity-powered machine, while slow to operate, could hurl a 300-lb (140-kg) rock several hundred feet.

Archers A rain of arrows from castle-top defenders forced attackers back.

Wall The incredibly thick stone wall was built smooth-faced and splayed at the bottom to hinder attackers.

Crenellation Battlements that offered shelter for defenders.

KEY

Attack

Defense

Infantry As most castles were eventually starved into submission rather than taken by direct assault, the infantry had to remain alert to prevent outside supplies being taken in.

Mangonel The torsion-powered siege engine, like a gigantic catapult, used a metal spring or, more usually, twisted horsehair.

Hoarding A temporary wooden structure with a high viewpoint, from which defenders could fire arrows.

Boiling water Defenders poured it onto enemies as they climbed the walls.

Tower By the 14th century, the strongest towers were clustered around the castle's weakest point, the gate.

Machicolation An opening through which attackers were assaulted with arrows or bombarded with hot oil and stones.

Throwing stones Heavy stones and missiles rained from the battlements onto the enemy below.

Loophole Narrow opening through which archers could shoot safely.

Belfry This wheeled tower enabled attackers to reach the top of the wall safely.

Ladder The simplest and quickest way of attacking a castle was to climb the walls using a ladder—the aim was to get a small party inside to open the gates.

Battering ram A large, heavy log, this basic weapon was used to attack walls and gates.

Pavise This wheeled, wooden shield protected attackers from enemy fire.

EXTREME TACTICS

BY CATAPULTING A DISEASE-RIDDEN BODY OVER THE WALLS, ASSAILANTS PUT THE DEFENDERS IN IMMEDIATE PERIL.

DEFENDERS OF A CASTLE COULD SNEAK UP ON THE ENEMY THROUGH A HIDDEN DOORWAY CALLED A SALLY PORT. THE DEFENDING SOLDIERS OF HADLEIGH CASTLE IN ESSEX, U.K., ARE SAID TO HAVE BOMBARDED THEIR ASSAILANTS WITH FRESH FISH THAT THEY HAD SMUGGLED IN.

IN 1306, SCOTLAND'S KILDRUMMY CASTLE FELL TO EDWARD, PRINCE OF WALES, WHEN OSBOURNE, THE TRAITOROUS BLACKSMITH, SET FIRE TO THE CASTLE GRAIN STORE.

IN 1204, FRENCH SOLDIERS TOOK CHÂTEAU GAILLARD FROM ENGLAND'S KING JOHN BY CLIMBING UP THE TOILET CHUTE.

Fame and FORTUNE

Human curiosity is the driving force behind many of history's greatest quests, discoveries, and adventures. People have explored to increase scientific knowledge, spread religious beliefs, gain riches and power, or just out of plain interest. However, many explorers are simply motivated by wealth and fame.

A NEW WORLD

In 1492, **Christopher Columbus** (1451–1506) set sail from Spain in an attempt to find a new route to Asia, to buy spices. When he found land, Columbus thought he'd reached Japan. In fact, he'd found a new continent—the Americas. Upon his return to Spain, the new continent became known as "the New World." In return for his many voyages of discovery, Columbus desired "great rewards" for both himself and his family.

Columbus

HIDDEN HOARD?

Edward Teach (c. 1680–1718), also known as **Blackbeard**, was a ruthless pirate renowned for his deliberately frightening appearance—he even wore slow-burning fuses under his hat. He ambushed and plundered ships in the Caribbean Sea and Atlantic Ocean until he was killed by the Royal Navy. Treasure seekers have since hunted high and low in the hope of finding Teach's legendary buried treasure.

Blackbeard

CUT SHORT

In 1519, Portuguese admiral **Ferdinand Magellan** (1480–1521) set out to travel westward around the world to the Spice Islands, sailing around South America and crossing the Pacific Ocean on the way. The landmark journey made Magellan famous, but he never lived to enjoy it—he was killed by Filipino warriors before his fleet reached its destination.

Magellan

GOLD DIGGER

Most educated Europeans in the 19th century had read Homer's *Iliad* and believed that Troy—one of the cities featured in the poem—was just a legend. From 1871–1873, businessman and amateur archeologist **Heinrich Schliemann** (1822–1890) uncovered the site of Troy at Hissarlik, Turkey. No fewer than nine different cities had been built and destroyed at this spot over the ages. Schliemann also uncovered a hoard of gold jewelry in the process.

EPIC JOURNEY

In *Il Milione*, an autobiographical account about the extraordinary travels of **Marco Polo** (c. 1254–1324), Polo stated that he had not mentioned one half of what he had seen because no one would believe him. In total, he traveled more than 25,000 mi (40,000 km) around the world and discovered many amazing inventions and innovations.

ONE LAST TRY

Howard Carter (1874–1939) was sure that the intact tomb of an ancient pharaoh lay somewhere in Egypt's Valley of the Kings. In 1922, after five years of exploration, Carter's patron, Lord Carnarvon, agreed to fund just one more season of excavation. It was enough —at the end of the year, Carter uncovered the most celebrated archeological find of all time—the tomb of Pharaoh Tutankhamun, untouched since 1327 BC.

PIRATE OR PATRIOT?

Sir Francis Drake (1540–1596) sailed round the world from 1577–1580, attacking Spanish treasure-laden vessels and pillaging their invaluable cargoes. On his return, Drake was hailed a hero and knighted by Queen Elizabeth I for his service to England. In Spain, however, Drake was deemed a murderous pirate.

Wonders
OF THE WORLD

We know about the Seven Wonders of the Ancient World from ancient Greek tourist guides. Historians are in disagreement over which monuments were on the list and even how many actually existed—we may never know for sure because only the Great Pyramid is still standing.

GREAT PYRAMID OF GIZA

WHAT: A giant stone tomb

WHERE: Near Cairo, Egypt

WHEN: Built during the reign of King Khufu (c. 2575-2465 BC)

SIZE: Base 755 sq ft (230 sq m); 480 ft (145 m) high

DESCRIPTION: Orientated on the four points of the compass and containing about 2.3 million limestone blocks, the pyramid was the tomb of King Khufu and his queen. The shape may have been chosen because it points to the sky—the domain of the sun god Ra.

DESCRIPTION: Described as being irrigated by an elaborate system of pumps and channels that brought water from the River Euphrates, the gardens were said to be a leisure feature of the royal palace. One legend says Nebuchadnezzar built them to remind his queen, Amytis, of the green forests of her Persian homeland.

WHAT: Remarkable terraced gardens

WHERE: In Babylon, the capital city of ancient Mesopotamia (now southern Iraq)

WHEN: During the reign of either Queen Sammuramat (810-783 BC) or King Nebuchadnezzar II (c. 605-561 BC)

SIZE: Unknown

STATUE OF ZEUS AT OLYMPIA

WHAT: A vast gold and ivory statue

WHERE: Olympia, in the Peloponnese, Greece

WHEN: Constructed by the sculptor Phidias around 430 BC

SIZE: 40 ft (12 m) high

DESCRIPTION: As the Olympic Games had deep religious significance, a temple to the king of the gods adorned the sporting complex. The statue of Zeus was shown seated, giving the impression that if he stood, he would burst through the roof.

HANGING GARDENS OF BABYLON

TEMPLE OF ARTEMIS AT EPHESUS

MAUSOLEUM OF MAUSOLUS AT HALICARNASSUS

DESCRIPTION:
Constructed of gleaming white marble, the Temple of Artemis was packed with works of art. Artemis (also known as Diana) was an ancient goddess of the moon. The temple was destroyed in AD 268, rebuilt, and finally razed in AD 401.

WHAT: A gigantic marble-columned temple

WHERE: Ephesus was in modern-day Turkey

WHEN: Built by King Croesus of Lydia c. 550 BC

SIZE: 350 ft (110 m) long, 180 ft (55 m) wide

DESCRIPTION: The gleaming tomb consisted of a plain rectangular base, topped with a colonnade, a pyramid roof, and a statue of Mausolus and Artemisia in a chariot pulled by four horses. It was built to demonstrate Artemisia's love for her Mausolus, and to glorify them both.

WHAT: A vast tomb shaped like a jewel box

WHERE: Overlooking the ancient city of Halicarnassus (now Bodrum), Turkey

WHEN: Built at the command of Queen Artemisia II of Caria, Mausolus' sister and widow, c. 353–350 BC

SIZE: Square base, with sides about 36 ft (11 m) long; 148 ft (45 m) tall

DESCRIPTION: The people of Rhodes erected this mighty bronze and iron statue of the sun god, Helios, to thank the deity for saving their city from enemy attack.

WHAT: A huge statue of a god beside the harbor entrance

WHERE: Mediterranean island of Rhodes, Greece

WHEN: Built 292–280 BC

SIZE: More than 107 ft (30 m) tall

PHAROS OF ALEXANDRIA

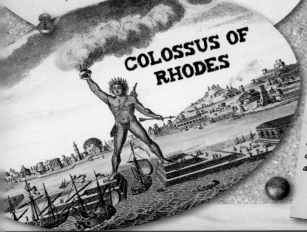

COLOSSUS OF RHODES

DESCRIPTION: The stone building rose in three tapering stages: square, octagonal, and cylindrical. The fire at the top was reflected in mirrors and visible 29 mi (47 km) away—it warned sailors of the treacherous banks around the Nile.

WHAT: The archetypal lighthouse

WHERE: Island of Pharos, Alexandria, Egypt

WHEN: Built 280–247 BC

SIZE: 350 ft (110 m) tall

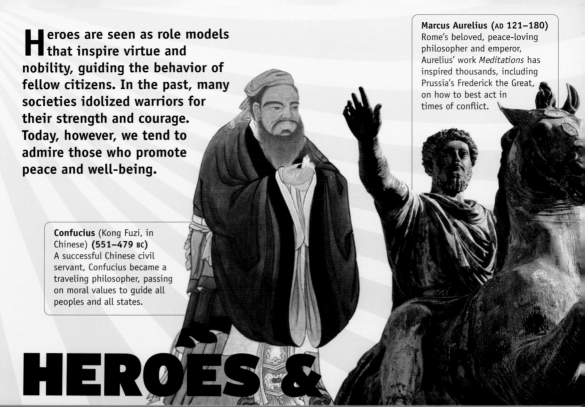

Heroes are seen as role models that inspire virtue and nobility, guiding the behavior of fellow citizens. In the past, many societies idolized warriors for their strength and courage. Today, however, we tend to admire those who promote peace and well-being.

Marcus Aurelius (AD 121–180) Rome's beloved, peace-loving philosopher and emperor, Aurelius' work *Meditations* has inspired thousands, including Prussia's Frederick the Great, on how to best act in times of conflict.

Confucius (Kong Fuzi, in Chinese) **(551–479 BC)** A successful Chinese civil servant, Confucius became a traveling philosopher, passing on moral values to guide all peoples and all states.

HEROES &

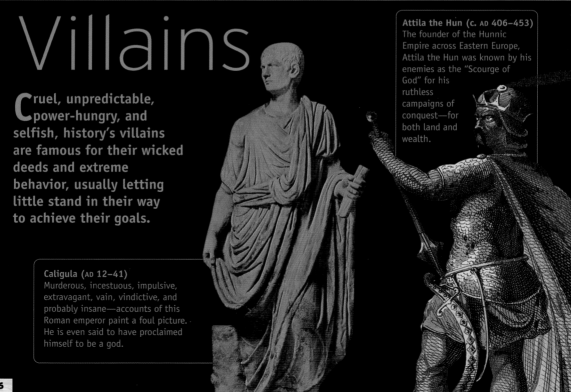

Villains

Cruel, unpredictable, power-hungry, and selfish, history's villains are famous for their wicked deeds and extreme behavior, usually letting little stand in their way to achieve their goals.

Attila the Hun (c. AD 406–453) The founder of the Hunnic Empire across Eastern Europe, Attila the Hun was known by his enemies as the "Scourge of God" for his ruthless campaigns of conquest—for both land and wealth.

Caligula (AD 12–41) Murderous, incestuous, impulsive, extravagant, vain, vindictive, and probably insane—accounts of this Roman emperor paint a foul picture. He is even said to have proclaimed himself to be a god.

Abraham Lincoln (1809–1865)
The 16th president of the United States, Lincoln led his nation through the American Civil War (1861–1865) and ended the country's slavery. He was assassinated in 1865 while attending a play with his wife.

Florence Nightingale (1820–1910)
Renowned for her work during the Crimean War (1853–1856), English nurse Nightingale cared for wounded soldiers, known to them as "the lady with the lamp" because she often made her rounds at night. She campaigned for nursing to be accepted as a profession for women.

Nelson Mandela (b. 1918)
In 1948, South Africa implemented a policy of apartheid (forced racial segregation). Mandela was a leader of the resistance movement, and became an international symbol of the fight for tolerance and equality. He was imprisoned for 27 years, and on his release became a respected statesman.

Genghis Khan (c. 1162–1227)
Born a simple tribal leader in northeast Asia, Khan united the nomadic tribes of Mongolia. The self-styled "Universal Ruler" carved out one of the largest empires the world has ever seen—by tireless campaigning and the heartless slaughter of local populations.

Ivan the Terrible (1530–1584)
Russia's first tsar, Ivan IV, became a corrupt and unstable tyrant who massacred thousands and even slew his own son in a fit of rage.

Joseph Stalin (1879–1953)
Born Iosif Dzhugashvili, the leader of the Soviet Union clawed his way to power and then retained the position by means of mass extermination—ordering the death and suffering of millions of people. Stalin is considered to be the force behind the biggest mass murder in history.

Great WARRIORS

Battles were won with the mind as much as muscle. First impressions counted, so warriors who looked intimidating and strong were often victorious. From medieval knights in shining armor to Viking marauders, history's finest fighting men were often extremely successful.

HOPLITE

Category: Citizen infantry
Place of operation: Ancient Greece
Dates: 8th–4th centuries BC
Headgear: Helmet with cheekplates
Body armor: Breastplate and greaves (leg armor), bronze cuirass or linen corselet
Weapons: 8-ft (3-m) spear and short sword
Shield: Round in shape, and made of wood and bronze
Discipline: Good
Notable success: Smashing Persian invasion at Marathon, 490 BC

VIKING

Category: Member of Nordic warrior band. Joined together in later centuries to form large armies
Place of operation: Europe, North Atlantic, and North America
Dates: 8th–11th century
Headgear: Steel helmet (without horns)
Body armor: Leather or chainmail tunic
Weapons: Spear, ax, sword, and dagger
Shield: Small and round. Made of wood or metal
Discipline: Poor
Notable success: Seizing the province of Rouen from the Kingdom of France in AD 911, and renaming it Normandy

ROMAN INFANTRY

Category: Professional foot soldier
Place of operation: Europe and the Near East
Dates: 2nd century BC–5th century AD
Headgear: Round, steel helmet with cheekplates
Body armor: Plates over upper body and shoulders
Weapons: 6-ft (2-m) javelin and short sword
Shield: Large, and (after 1st century AD) rectangular and curved. Made of plywood reinforced with bronze or iron
Discipline: Excellent
Notable success: Conquest of Britain, 1st century AD

MEDIEVAL KNIGHT

Category: Gentleman warrior
Place of operation: Europe and Middle East
Dates: 11th–15th century
Headgear: Varies according to the period—among the most well known was a style of helmet that totally enclosed the head, called the great helm
Body armor: In later years, full plate armor (made from plates of metal) worn over chainmail
Weapons: 13-ft (4-m) lance, heavy sword, ax, and dagger
Shield: All shapes, made of wood and steel
Discipline: Poor
Notable success: In the Battle of Arsuf in 1191, Richard the Lionheart defeated Saladin

AZTEC SOLDIER

Category: Citizen army spearheaded by professional nobility
Place of operation: Central America
Dates: 14th–16th century
Headgear: Quilted cotton helmet, often highly decorated
Body armor: Quilted cotton suit covering most of the body
Weapons: Wooden javelins and clubs, bows and arrows, knives made of a razor-sharp stone called obsidian
Shield: Wooden and feather-fringed
Discipline: Average
Notable success: Victory over Azcapotzalco in 1428

SAMURAI

Category: Military nobility
Place of operation: Japan
Dates: 12th–19th centuries
Head gear: Metal helmet splayed to protect neck; sometimes with face mask
Body armour: Elaborate combination of metal, bamboo, and quilted cloth covering the entire body
Weapons: *Katana* sword, club, bow, spear, knife, and firearms
Shield: Where carried, round in shape. Made of wood and metal
Discipline: Good
Notable success: Japanese invasion of Korea, 1592–1593

ZULU WARRIOR

Category: Tribal infantryman
Place of operation: Southern Africa
Dates: 18th and 19th centuries
Headgear: Circlet of animal pelt
Body armor: None
Weapons: Spears—the *isijula* for throwing and the *iklwa* for stabbing—and club
Shield: Leaf shaped, and made of animal hide
Discipline: High
Notable success: Defeat of British at Isandlwana in 1879

LOST **LEADERS**

Throughout history, the lives of many key figures—popular and unpopular—have been brought to an untimely close. Assassinations are targeted killings, usually motivated by political differences, but may also be driven by religious beliefs, military opposition, or monetary gain.

French King Henry IV

Fanaticism knows no bounds, as France's popular King Henry IV (1553–1610) discovered in 1610. Born a Protestant, he converted to Catholicism and, to heal his country's religious divisions, granted toleration to those of his former faith. All this was too much for François Ravaillac, who stabbed the king to death when the royal carriage was stopped in busy traffic on the way to the queen's coronation.

Roman general Julius Caesar

The career of one of Rome's greatest generals and reformers, Julius Caesar (100–44 BC), came to an abrupt end on March 15, 44 BC, when he was stabbed to death in the Senate House. The assassins' motive? To save the Roman republic from a would-be king.

ENGLISH KING WILLIAM II

William II (c. 1056–1100) was not one of England's more popular kings. Tongues began to wag, therefore, when he went hunting in the New Forest and did not return. His body, pierced by an arrow, was found the next morning—and his brother Henry immediately seized the throne. Was the king's death an accident, or assassination?

Russian Tsar Alexander II

For all his reforming zeal, notably setting free his country's serfs in 1861, Russian Tsar Alexander II (1818–1881) did not go far enough for the People's Will, an extreme terrorist organization. Whether the people willed it or not, the gang's assassins killed the tsar in a bomb attack as he rode in his carriage through the streets of St. Petersburg.

Austro-Hungarian Archduke Franz Ferdinand

On June 28, 1914, the Serbian nationalist Gavrilo Princip fired two fatal shots in Sarajevo, Bosnia, that started World War I (1914–1918). His victim was the Austro-Hungarian prince, Archduke Franz Ferdinand. Austria soon attacked Serbia. Russia came to the aid of its Serbian ally, and Germany did the same with Austria. France, Russia's ally, was drawn in next... and within weeks a whole continent, then the whole world, was at war.

JFK moments before the shooting took place.

U.S. President John F. Kennedy

As U.S. President John F. Kennedy was driving through Dallas, Texas, U.S., on November 22, 1963, at precisely 12:30 p.m. four shots were fired. The president, hit in the body and head, died shortly afterward. A suspect, Lee Harvey Oswald, was arrested but shot dead before he was brought to trial. So one of modern history's great mysteries began—who killed JFK and why?

Israeli President Yitzhak Rabin

Israel and its Arab neighbors have long been at each other's throats. So when Yitzhak Rabin (1922–1995) signed the Oslo Accords with the Palestinians in 1993, he was awarded the Nobel Prize for Peace. Two years later, he was assassinated by Israeli Yigal Amir who opposed the agreement.

Security agents push Rabin into a car after he was shot in Tel Aviv after addressing a peace rally.

Wipe OUT!

It came from the east, spreading like a wave of death across Europe. In just four years (1347–1351), half of the continent's population was wiped out. Rich and poor, men and women... no one was immune from the bubonic plague, also known as the Great Plague or the "Black Death." Although population levels recovered surprisingly swiftly, the continent would never be the same again.

Spread of death

The Black Death, first brought to Europe by rats aboard vessels sailing from the Eastern Mediterranean, persisted for more than 400 years. Its name came from its most obvious symptoms—pus-oozing, black swellings, called buboes, under the arms, on the neck, and in the groin. Those infected had a one-in-five chance of survival—the majority were dead within a week.

Dirty rats

Most scientists believe the plague was spread by fleas that lived on black rats. In an age when basic hygiene was almost nonexistent, rat fleas flourished in bedding and clothing. It took just one flea bite to infect a person. Modern medics, however, have suggested that the disease was actually caused by a bacterium called *Yersinia pestis*.

▼ This grim depiction shows how people were dying in the street, leaving piles of diseased bodies.

Doctor, doctor

At a time when some doctors believed the plague could be spread by just looking at someone, so-called "cures" were bizarre. They included swallowing emeralds, pearls, or gold, placing dried human excrement on the buboes, and drinking a mixture of apple syrup, lemon, rose water, and peppermint.

▶ Doctors wore "plague-proof" clothing." The "beak" acted like a gas mask, stopping them from inhaling air that may carry the plague when treating victims.

ONE MEDIEVAL REMEDY FOR THE PLAGUE WAS TO DRINK A GLASS OF YOUR OWN URINE TWICE A DAY.

Death, the "Grim Reaper," with his scythe.

Mass graves

The bodies of plague victims had to be disposed of as quickly as possible, otherwise the bodies would rot and spread further disease. With so many deaths, individual funerals were impossible. Corpses were simply collected in carts and dumped in mass graves.

► Hundreds of dead bodies were buried in pits.

Heaven's judgment

In a fiercely religious age, the plague was seen as God's judgment on a wicked world. Prevention and cure came not from science, but from prayer, confession, and penance.

▼ More than 1,000 bodies were discovered in Black Death graves near the Tower of London, England, in 1987.

Flagellation (beating or whipping the body) was believed to atone for the sins that had brought the plague.

On and on...

Evidence of the dreadful Black Death has come from the excavation of mass graves. Outbreaks of this terrifying epidemic have also occured in modern times—as recently as 1994 there was an outbreak in Seurat, India.

Supreme
SACRIFICE

The early gods were a grim bunch. Erratic and demanding, a number of them could be appeased only with the ultimate sacrifice—human life. No one did this in a more spectacularly gory fashion than the Aztec people of what is now southern Mexico.

▲ An Aztec priest cuts out the beating heart of a prisoner of war and holds it up to the sun god.

Burning basket

When campaigning in Northern Europe, Julius Caesar described how Celtic druids pleased their gods with human sacrifice. He reported that they had built a huge, wickerwork statue, imprisoned people within it, and then set fire to the structure.

▶ According to Caesar, the criminal and innocent alike were sacrificed within the large, wicker statue.

Heart of the matter

The Aztecs believed that Huitzilopochtli, the god of war and sun, needed a regular supply of blood to sustain him in his battle with darkness. Therefore, on festive days, prisoners of war were taken to the sacrificial altar atop the pyramid temple in Tenochtitlan, the capital of the Aztec Empire. Here, the hearts of victims were cut out in a bloody ritual.

Sati is the ancient Hindu custom of burning a bereaved wife on the funeral pyre of her dead husband.

Pyre power

The Hindu ritual, Sati, demanded that a wife be burned to death, voluntarily or otherwise, on the funeral pyre of her dead husband. It was believed that the custom arose to stop young wives poisoning elderly and unwanted husbands.

Pleasing Thor

According to the medieval German chronicler Adam of Bremen, the ancient temple at Uppsala, Sweden, witnessed some pretty grim events. The worship of Thor and other Norse gods and goddesses involved ritual human sacrifice.

The Nordic King Domalde prepares to sacrifice himself for the good of his people.

GREEK MYTHS TELL HOW EVERY SEVEN YEARS THE ATHENIANS SENT 14 CHILDREN TO BE EATEN BY THE MINOTAUR, A TERRIFYING MONSTER.

A Japanese kamikaze plane attempts to smash into a U.S. warship.

Divine wind

The term "kamikaze," meaning "divine wind," was originally used to describe the tropical typhoons that broke up Chinese invasion fleets heading for Japan in the late 13th century. In World War II, the term was adopted by Japanese suicide pilots who deliberately smashed their planes into U.S. warships—about 2,800 kamikaze attacks sank or crippled hundreds of ships.

FANCY DRESS

As soon as our ancestors started wearing clothing more than 100,000 years ago, they wanted to look good. Most garments were attractive and designed to accentuate the wearer's best features. But at the extremes, people's fashion obsessions became peculiar—for example, women piling their hair 12 in (30 cm) high. Some fashion trends were even cruel, such as the Chinese practice of binding girls' feet so they could fit into shoes many sizes too small for them.

◄▼ The toga was both a garment and a badge of citizenship.

Roman robe

The toga of ancient Rome was much more than a simple 20-ft- (6-m-) long robe of fine wool, draped around the body and slung over the shoulder. It also showed the wearer place in society—by law, the garment could be worn only by ma citizens of Rome.

◄ Proud of a shapely leg, 16th-century men wore tights to show theirs off.

Elizabethan costume

Shakespeare's theater company's most valuable possession was its wardrobe of costumes. Not surprisingly, it cost more than most Elizabethans earned in a year to dress a gentleman in a lined, embroidered doublet (jacket) with detachable sleeves, neck ruff, padded tights over the upper thigh and silk stockings below, and elegant shoes.

Geisha girls

Since the 18th century, highly trained Japanese Geisha have been used for entertainment. With a chalk-white face, scarlet lips, hair decorated with flowers, an elegant kimono, a brilliant obi (sash), and platform shoes, a Geisha captivated her guests with elaborate dance and music.

◄ Geishas still work today, attending parties and gatherings.

Aristocratic excess

Late 18th-century European dress is a fabulous example of fashion at its most extreme. A lady's gown ballooned like a bell from her tiny waist, and the puffed sleeves were trimmed with ruffles. The hairdo, many times the size of the wearer's head, looked like a bird had made its nest atop the entire extraordinary collection.

► Costumes in the 18th century were low at the front and high on the head.

▼ The marked faces of New Zealand's Maori warriors made them look ferocious.

Bone-cut beauty

The Maori people of New Zealand boasted a long tradition of Tā moko, marking the body permanently with incisions and natural dyes. Carved with bone chisels, the markings were used to indicate power and authority. They appeared most commonly on the face, thighs, and buttocks.

Remarkable rears

Late 19th-century fashion designers created bustle dresses that expanded so much at the rear, they had to be supported by steel cages.

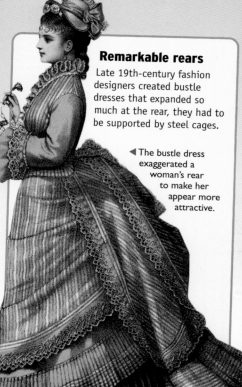

◄ The bustle dress exaggerated a woman's rear to make her appear more attractive.

Eagle signals

When in battle, an opponent knew immediately whether to fight or flee from a Native American Sioux, Crow, Blackfeet, Cheyenne, or Plains Cree warrior. Each eagle feather in the striking warbonnet of a warrior represented an act of outstanding bravery. Lots of feathers? Get out of the way—fast!

◄ The feathers in the warbonnet of Sitting Bull, the war chief of the Sioux, continued down his back.

RAT-atouille

Humans are omnivorous—we eat both plants and meat. During the reign of England's James I (1603–1625), starving soldiers resorted to sharing the diet of their cows—grass. At the other extreme, Henry VIII (1491–1547) sat down to vast feasts of hare, venison, veal, chicken, plums, and pomegranate seeds... and that was just the first course!

DURING THE CIVIL WAR THAT FOLLOWED THE RUSSIAN REVOLUTION OF 1917, STARVING PEASANTS WERE PHOTOGRAPHED SELLING HUMAN FLESH FOR PEOPLE TO EAT.

GREEDY ROMANS SOMETIMES MADE THEMSELVES SICK IN ORDER TO BE ABLE TO EAT MORE.

Extreme generosity

In 1900, the French government employed 3,600 cooks and waiters to prepare a feast for the country's mayors that featured, among other things, more than 2 tons of pheasant and 50,000 bottles of wine. *Bon appétit!*

Hand to mouth

For most of history, people used knives to cut meat and spoons to scoop up liquid, but they generally used their fingers to transfer food to their mouths. Fine if your hands are clean...

LITTLE LUXURY

Ancient Romans were partial to a mid-morning snack, and one of their favorite nibbles was a crunchy edible dormouse.

A feast of beasts

Chronicles say that around 484 BC, King Darius of Persia had 1,000 animals slaughtered for a special feast. The menu was said to have included smoked camel, ox, zebra, and ostrich.

Big bird

Until the 17th century, swan was a popular dish among the wealthiest in society. The bird was roasted for a long time and served "like beef."

Raise a glass?

Before the late 16th century, most Europeans drank their tipple from pewter, pottery, or leather. Drinking vessels made from leather were lined with resin to make them watertight.

Boozy breakfast

In medieval times, water and milk frequently carried diseases. To avoid illness, those who could afford to drank beer and wine at all times of the day and night.

Fitting the CRIME

The ancient Athenians devised a fail-safe way of dealing with those who were regarded as a political nuisance. A meeting of citizens was called, at which all present wrote on a potsherd (a fragment of pottery, called an *ostrakon*) the name of anyone they wished to remove. Anyone receiving a large number of votes was ostracized—banished from the state for ten years.

▼ The name of an unpopular Athenian citizen is scratched onto a piece of pottery.

L egal systems claim that a person's punishment should fit their crime. Yet from hanging for stealing a sheep to crushing bones for lifting a loaf, the past is littered with examples of extreme punishments given out for apparently trivial crimes.

Off with his head

One of the most shocking punishments took place during the French Revolution's Reign of Terror (1793–1794). Once the revolutionary leader Maximilien Robespierre had defined the crime—being an enemy of the people, and the punishment—death, thousands of men and women were guillotined for the crime of simply being who they were. An aristocrat, for instance, was by definition an enemy of the people.

▶ In the late 18th century, the iron maiden was used as a form of torture. The victim was shut inside the cabinet and pierced with sharp objects.

In 1793, Marie Antoinette was executed by guillotine for treason.

TOOLS OF TORTURE

Torture has long been a means of extracting information from a person—usually using brutal methods. There was no question of punishments fitting the crime for slaves in ancient Rome. In the pre-Christian era, slaves accused of a crime, even a minor one, were automatically tortured—it was seen as the only way of getting the truth out of them. Harsher still, in imperial times, when a slave was found guilty of murder, it was quite common for all other slaves belonging to the same master to be crucified.

CHOP CHOP

English puritan William Prynne (1600–1669) believed the theater to be unlawful and immoral, and set out his ideas in the 1,000-page book *Histriomastix* (1632). Shortly after the book appeared, Queen Henrietta Maria appeared in a private court drama. In light of this, parts of *Histriomastix* were interpreted as an attack on the queen. Prynne was fined, imprisoned, and punished by having his ears sliced.

Prynne was put in the pillory—a wooden frame—to have the tips of his ears chopped off.

IN ANCIENT CHINA, THE PUNISHMENT FOR KILLING A PARENT, EVEN ACCIDENTALLY, WAS EXECUTION. BUT A FATHER WHO BEAT HIS SON TO DEATH WOULD USUALLY RECEIVE NO MORE THAN A FINE.

▼ Many women were burned at the stake from the 15th to 18th century, after being found guilty of witchcraft.

▼ In medieval times, the neck and hands of offenders would be locked between two wooden planks—the pillory—in a public place, so they could be humiliated.

▶ The "Chair of Torture" was covered in spikes along the back, seat, and arms. The spikes would penetrate the flesh, causing slow blood loss, and eventual death.

The last witch

In 1782, Anna Göldi of the Swiss town of Glarus was executed by decapitation. She had confessed under torture to having seen the Devil in the form of a black dog, and that it had helped her put needles into the food of her master's daughters. She was the last person to be executed for witchcraft in Europe.

Cure
OR KILL

Until the scientific revolution of the late 17th century, most medicine was a mix of superstition, religion, folklore, myth, trickery, and guesswork. "Cures" included rubbing the affected part of the body with a live toad (a treatment for the plague), drinking a cup of tea made from ground-up insects (antirabies medicine), and dressing a wound with a scribe's excrement and milk. Many so-called treatments did more harm than good, and those who stayed out of the hands of doctors often had the best chance of survival!

MEDIEVAL MEDICINE WAS BASED ON THE IDEA THAT THE BODY CONTAINED FOUR "HUMORS"—BLACK BILE, YELLOW BILE, PHLEGM, AND BLOOD. AN EXCESS OF BLACK BILE, FOR EXAMPLE, WAS THOUGHT TO PRODUCE MELANCHOLY.

FEELING THE HEAT

A person suffering from toothache in medieval Europe may be instructed to hold a lit candle close to the affected area. Apparently this would cause the worms that were eating away the inside of the tooth to drop out into a waiting cup.

Burning away the badness: curing toothache with a lit candle.

▼ Cure by hot cups in a German bathhouse.

TOXIN TREATMENT

The traditional treatment of placing hot cups on the skin has been used since the time of the ancient Egyptians. This "cure" is intended to draw unwanted fluids from the body as the air inside the cups cools and contracts. The procedure creates circular marks on the skin and has no proven benefits.

Cups are still used today in alternative medicine.

PENNY DREADFUL

Not until modern times was mental illness properly recognized or treated. Until the 19th century, London's Bethlem Royal Hospital (once known as Bedlam) was a kind of freak show where visitors paid a penny to gawp at unfortunate "mad" inmates held in chains.

◀ The well-dressed women in this scene from *A Rake's Progress* by 18th-century English artist William Hogarth are visiting Bedlam (London's hospital for the mentally ill) as entertainment.

elf-medication with the of bloodsucking leeches.

LOSING A LIMB

A mangled or seriously septic limb is better off than on. But before the invention of anesthetic, such operations (usually performed with dirty knives or saws) often led to the conscious patient's immediate death—from shock.

This may hurt a bit... amputation, 17th-century style.

BLOODSUCKERS

Many prescientific societies believed that removing blood from the body, either via an incision into a vein or by drawing it out using leeches, helped to cure illness. In fact, apart from temporarily relieving high blood pressure, this treatment made the patient worse.

DOCTOR TOAD

In medieval times people wore small bags around their necks. Inside would be a dustlike substance, which was believed to ward off all kinds of illnesses, even cancer. The "miracle" cure? Dried and powdered toad.

Get ready to grind: powdered toad acts as a "miracle" cure.

Hole in the head

All over the world, from prehistoric times onward, head injuries, migraines, and even depression were treated by "trepanning"—an operation in which a hole up to 2 in (5 cm) across was drilled in the skull to relieve pressure or let out excess fluid. The procedure did save some lives, but the risk of death by fatal infection or surgeon's error was high.

◄ Trepanning caused as many headaches as it cured.

An unlucky patient with a holey head.

There have always been rich and poor people, but when the Industrial Revolution began in the mid-18th century—first in Britain, then spreading to Europe, North America, and eventually the rest of the world—this gulf became more obvious. Workers who swarmed into cities lived in makeshift, squalid housing, while across the ocean, transported Africans endured even worse conditions as unpaid slaves. All the while, thousands of mill and mine owners, bankers, shippers, and builders were growing rich beyond their wildest dreams.

All in one room

Until the 20th century, it was quite common for European working-class families to have no more than a single room to live in. The situation was especially bad in the rapidly expanding industrial cities.

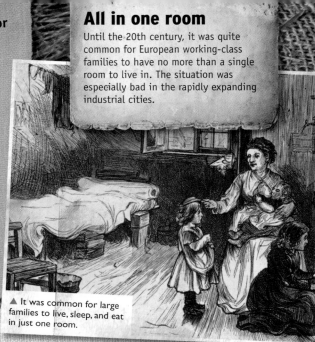

▲ It was common for large families to live, sleep, and eat in just one room.

SLUMDOGS and

MILLIONAIRES

Royal riches

Queen Victoria received £385,000 a year from the British government just for being queen. That's equivalent to £21 million, or $34 million in today's money. When she died in 1901, she left a fortune of over £2 million (about £24 million, or $50 million today).

THE DUKE OF PORTLAND HAD A 1.5-MI (2.4-KM) UNDERGROUND TUNNEL BUILT SO HE COULD TRAVEL FROM HIS HOME (WELBECK ABBEY, U.K.) TO THE RAILWAY STATION AT WORKSOP WITHOUT BEING SEEN.

NO EXPENSE SPARED— THE CORONATION OF QUEEN VICTORIA (1838) COST £70,000.

Paupers' palaces

Too poor to support yourself? Off to the workhouse! These bleak establishments housed the poor and their children, providing low-grade shelter and food in return for soul-destroying labor. With prisonlike rules and punishments, workhouses were kept deliberately unpleasant to deter scroungers.

▼ Paupers sit down to a meager meal in the Marylebone workhouse in London, U.K.

▼ Factory workers lived in rows of small houses, with no inside bathrooms or running water. The air was dirty, filled with smoke from the nearby factories.

Dirty work

Many factories were built during the Industrial Revolution, and both adults and children had to work long hours in unhealthy conditions. Until 1850, only the factory owners benefited from the wealth generated by industry, with the workers living in dirty, crowded, busy towns, called slums, that sprang up around the factories.

Dazzling display

In 1849, Queen Victoria's husband, Prince Albert, conceived a plan for a global exhibition to take place in London. The exhibition opened on May 1, 1851, with more than 14,000 people gathered in the newly built Crystal Palace to show off their gadgets to millions of dazzled visitors. By the time the exhibition closed, one quarter of the British population had visited Crystal Palace.

LONDON'S CRYSTAL PALACE (1851) WAS A SYMBOL OF THE INDUSTRIAL REVOLUTION THAT MADE SOME BRITONS FABULOUSLY WEALTHY.

WAR AND PEACE

Prince of peace

Horrified by the 100,000 casualties resulting from the Kalinga War (c. 265 BC), the great Indian emperor Ashoka (304–232 BC) converted to Buddhism and inaugurated one of the most peaceful, fair, and tolerant reigns history has ever witnessed. Education, health, justice, welfare—every branch of government felt the touch of his nonviolent outlook. After Ashoka's death, he was remembered as Samraat Chakravartin—the Emperor of Emperors.

Humans, said the poet Alexander Pope, are "The glory, jest, and riddle of the world"—and never more so than in matters of war and peace. After the horrors of World War I (1914–1918), monuments to peace went up all over Europe; yet barely 20 years later the continent was tearing itself apart once again. Although many of history's most celebrated figures were promoters of peace, we also have a fascination with the heroic (and sometimes barbaric) deeds of warriors and military leaders.

A reputation for destruction

Hollywood has made a pretty good job of portraying the Roman Empire as a place of war and gratuitous violence, but this picture is unfair. For over 200 years (AD 27–180) the empire fought few major wars and spread a relatively civilized blanket of law and order across the Mediterranean world, over which it held sway.

▼ Many people's views of the Roman Empire are informed by movies such as *Gladiator* (2000), which emphasize its violence rather than its imposition of law and order.

Land grab

In 1066, William of Normandy seized the English crown and so began a conflict that finally ended in 1558, when Calais, England's last continental possession, fell to the French. Essentially, the struggle was dynastic—fueled by kings trying to expand their territories by force rather than ethical issues. This unworthy conflict reached its climax in the Hundred Years' War (which actually lasted for 116 years, 1337–1453).

◀ French, Spanish, and English forces battle for power at Nájera, in 1367.

Stacks of skulls

The central Asian conqueror Tamerlane (1336–1405) specialized in acts of extreme barbarity. While carving out an empire around Persia and the Caspian Sea, his forces may have killed 100,000 innocent citizens in a single day. On a more personal note, he took pleasure in firing human heads from cannon, and built huge pyramids from the skulls of his victims.

▶ Ruthless conqueror Tamerlane was also known as "Amir Timur" or (inaccurately) "Timur the Great."

Ultimate weapon

On August 6, 1945, the atom bomb nicknamed "Little Boy" obliterated the Japanese city of Hiroshima, and humankind saw that it now had the power to destroy itself and the planet on which it lived. U.S. President Harry S. Truman had thought long and hard about using the bomb, eventually deciding that dropping it would, in the long run, save lives. We all live with the consequences of that decision.

▲ Hiroshima, 1945: the utter devastation provides a stark warning to humanity.

Crazy ACTS

When Mr. Bumble declared in Charles Dickens' *Oliver Twist*, "The law is an ass!" he was not so far off the mark. History is littered with ill-considered laws, and while some were merely foolish, others were downright nasty. An English law banning entry into Parliament in full armor might have made sense in 1313, but was still on the statute book in 2011. A law passed in 1908 in the U.S. state of Oklahoma banned marriage between a "person of African descent" and "any person not of African descent."

Lean and mean

Debates about obesity often present it as a modern issue. However, an English law of 1336, designed to prevent the population from becoming fat and unfit, made it illegal to eat more than two courses at a single meal.

The "Rich Kitchen" by Jan van der Heyden, 1563

Crazy cabs

The rules and regulations for taxicabs are very specific. In London, U.K., it is illegal to hail a taxicab if you are suffering from the plague. Furthermore, it is forbidden for a taxicab to carry corpses or rabid dogs.

Single or married?

In Florida, U.S., an unmarried woman may face jail if she parachutes on a Sunday. In Vermont, U.S., a husband must give written permission for his wife to be allowed to wear false teeth.

Dressing up

Lawmakers love to interfere in daily life, especially when it comes to dress. The Italian capital Rome banned low-cut dresses during the 16th century, and in Massachusetts, U.S., a law of 1651 outlawed the wearing of gold or silver buttons, lace, and other finery by anyone not worth at least £200.

Mulberry madness

China ferociously guarded its hold over the immensely profitable silk industry, and punished anyone who let slip the top-secret processes involved. One law stated that any person who revealed how the cocoons of the larvae of the mulberry silkworm were harvested and turned into thread would be put to death by torture.

Loony law

A law allegedly passed by an absentminded U.S. state of Florida legislature in the 1960s made it illegal to carry firearms "except for the purpose of shooting vermin or policemen in the course of their duty." The wording was amended before a law officer was harmed.

The power of names

Although he was an undemocratic dictator, the people of France had huge admiration for Emperor Napoleon I (1769–1821)—so much so that they made it illegal to name a pig after him. The move inspired English writer George Orwell to use the name for the tyrannous pig in his book *Animal Farm* (1945).

▼ Black passengers on a South African train give the thumbs up from a carriage that was previously reserved for white people only.

SLEGS BLANKES
EUROPEANS ONLY

Racist rot

Having legislated to define everyone by their race, in 1950 the South African government passed a law (the Group Areas Act) stipulating where members of each racial group were allowed to live. Needless to say, the white sections of society, who had made the law, were allocated the best areas.

INDEX

Entries in **bold** refer to main subject entries; entries in *italics* refer to illustrations.

acts (laws) **38–9**
Albert, Prince 35
Alexander II (Tsar of Russia) 21, *21*
Alexander the Great 8
amputation 33, *33*
Animal Farm 39
animals, in wartime **8–9**, *8*, *9*
apartheid 39
archers 10
armor 18–19, *18–19*
Ashoka 36
assassination 17, **20–1**
atomic bombs 37, *37*
Attila the Hun 16, *16*
Aurelius, Marcus 16, *16*
Aztecs
    sacrifices 24, *24*
    soldiers 19, *19*

Balaclava, Battle of *9*
battering rams *11*
battlements 10
belfries *11*
Bethlehem Royal Hospital
    (Bedlam) 32, *32*
Blackbeard (Edward Teach) 12, *12*
Black Death **22–3**, *22–3*
bubonic plague **22–3**, *22–3*

Caesar, Julius 20, *20*, 24
Caligula 16, *16*
camels 8, *8–9*, *9*
canopic jars 6, *6*
carrier pigeons *9*
Carter, Howard 13, *13*
castles **10–11**, *10–11*
cats, mummified 7, *7*
cavalries 9, *9*
Celtic druids 24, *24*
Château Gaillard, France 11
clothes **26–7**, *26–7*, 38
coffins 7, *7*
Colossus of Rhodes 15, *15*
Columbus, Christopher 12, *12*
Confucius 16, *16*
crenellations 10
Crystal Palace 35, *35*
cup cure 32, *32*

doctors, plague 22, *22*
dogs
    in wartime 9, *9*
    mummified 7, *7*
Drake, Francis 13, *13*
druids 24, *24*

Egyptians, ancient 6–7
elephants 8, *8*
Elizabethan costume 26, *26*
European dress (late 18th
    century) 27, *27*
explorers **12–13**, *12–13*

factory workers' houses 35, *35*
fashion **26–7**
Ferdinand, Franz (Archduke of
    Austro-Hungarian Empire) 21,
    21
flagellation *23*
fleas 22
foot binding 26

Geisha girls 26, *26*
Gladiator (film) *36*
Great Plague **22–3**
Great Pyramid of Giza 14, *14*
gun laws 39

Hadleigh Castle, U.K. 11
Hanging Gardens of Babylon 14,
    14
Hannibal *8*
Henry IV (King of France) 20, *20*
heroes **16–17**, *16–17*
Hinduism 25
Hiroshima 37, *37*
hoardings *11*
Hoplites 18, *18–19*
horses 8, *9*, *9*
houses 35, *35*
Hundred Years' War 37

Imperial Camel Corps *8–9*, *9*
Industrial Revolution **35–6**
infantry 10
Ivan the Terrible 17, *17*

Japan
    Geisha girls 26, *26*
    Hiroshima 37, *37*
    kamikaze pilots 25, *25*

Kalinga War 36
kamikaze pilots 25, *25*
Kennedy, John F. 21, *21*
Khan, Genghis 17, *17*
Kildrummy Castle, U.K. 11
knights 19, *19*

laws **38–9**
leeches 32
Lincoln, Abraham 17, *17*
loopholes *11*

machicolations *11*
Magellan, Ferdinand 12, *12*
Mandela, Nelson 17, *17*
mangonels 10
Maori people 27, *27*
mass graves 23, *23*
Mausoleum of Mausolus 15,
    15
medicine **32–3**
medieval knights 19, *19*
medieval medicine 32
mental illness 32, *32*
Minotaur of Athens 25
Monguls 8
mulberry silkworms 39, *39*
mummification **6–7**

Nájara, battle at *37*
Napoleon I 39
Native Americans 27, *27*
natron 7, *7*
New Zealand
    Maoris 27, *27*
Nightingale, Florence 17, *17*

obesity laws 38
Orwell, George 39
Oswald, Lee Harvey 21

pavise *11*
peace **36–7**
Pharos of Alexandria 15, *15*
pigeons *9*
plague **22–3**
Polo, Marco 13
Pope, Alexander 36
Portland, Duke of 34
Princip, Gavrilo 21, *21*
Pyramid of Giza 14, *14*

Rabin, Yitzhak 21, *21*
racism 39
rats 22, *22*
Ravaillac, François 20, *20*
Rich Kitchen 38
Roman
    clothes 26, *26*
    Empire 36, *36*
    infantry 18, *18*

sacrifice **24–5**
Samurai 19, *19*
Sati 25, *25*
Schliemann, Heinrich 13
Seven Wonders of the World
    14–15, *14–15*
sieges **10–11**, *10–11*
silk industry 39
Sitting Bull 27
slaves 34
slums 35
South Africa 17, 39
Stalin, Joseph 17, *17*
Statue of Zeus 14, *14*

Tamerlane 37, *37*
Teach, Edward (Blackbeard) 12,
    12
Temple of Artemis 15, *15*
toads, as medieval cure 33
togas 26, *26*
toothache cure 32
trebuchets 10
trepanning 33, *33*
Troy 13, *13*
Truman, Harry S. 37
Tutankhamun 13, *13*

Victoria, Queen 34, *34*
Vikings 18, *18–19*
villains **16–17**, *16–17*

war **36–7**
warriors **18–19**, *18–19*

weapons 18–19, *18–19*
wicker statue 24, *24*
William II (King of England) 20,
    20
William of Normandy 37
Wonders of the World **14–15**,
    14–15
workhouses 35, *35*
World War I 21

Zeus, statue of 14, *14*
Zulu warriors 19, *19*